Loving the Love of Your Life

Show Her How Much You Really Care

(And See What Happens Next!)

Loving the Love of Your Life

Thomas Nelson, Inc. titles may be purchased in bulk for educational,
business, fund-raising, or sales promotional use. For information,
please e-mail SpecialMarkets@ThomasNelson.com.

Project Editor: Mark Gilroy Creative, LLC

Designed by Thinkpen Design, Inc., www.thinkpendesign.com

ISBN-13: 978-1-4041-8764-1

Printed and bound in the United States of America

www.thomasnelson.com

Table of Contents

Introduction
For Husbands Only

(No peeking, ladies.)

When you look around at your friends' and family's marriages and at your own, you realize that marriages are as different as the people in them. But whether a couple is blissfully happy or on the brink of disaster, there's one thing every marriage has in common: room for improvement. Love must be nurtured if it's going to thrive and grow—every single day.

That's where this book comes in. Because love isn't really a feeling as much as a practice. And by practicing love, you enable the love-feelings to grow deeper. Along the way, mutual trust and respect are built up; resentments crumble and give way to forgiveness; and a climate of love and appreciation begins to form—all markers of a happy and stable marriage. We hope to give you tools and ideas for loving the love of your life practically and actively, getting you on the road to the marriage you long for.

As you get started, here are some simple guidelines to follow:

1. If you're going through it with your wife, take turns reading and doing the activities in each chapter, using your own creativity to add to or modify an activity any way you'd

like. Read the "Know It" section, take the action step in the "Show It" section, then give the book back to your wife by following the instructions in the "Pass It On" section. Now it's her turn. Don't pick up the book again until she passes it back to you. And no flipping the book over and peeking at activities she might have planned for you.

2. If you're working through this book on your own, don't lose heart—one person's efforts in a marriage can go a long, long way, even if they're not immediately reciprocated.

3. Go for it. Some of these activities might seem a little goofy, maybe a little high-school. But try to let go of mundane adult seriousness and just go for it! A little goofiness might be just what you need to rekindle that youthful spark you felt when you were dating.

4. There's one more guideline for using this book, and it's critical: no peeking! Okay, that's been mentioned, but we know it's tempting. Those fuchsia-colored pages are just a short finger-walk away from your side of the book, and wouldn't it be nice to know what she is cooking up? But you'll appreciate your wife's activities better if you receive them without expectation. Let yourself be surprised, and let your wife surprise you.

So turn the page to the first chapter and settle down in your chair to read and make plans for showing the one you love that you love her. She won't know what hit her—and neither will your marriage. ❤

Take an Active Interest in Her Day

*Let each of you look out
not only for his own interests,
but also for the interests of others.*

KNOW IT

At the end of the workday, there are two common ways to communicate when you first get home. One is to recap your day at work—the good, the bad, and the ugly. And there's a good chance your wife wants you to debrief your day that way. A second option is to come home and shut everybody out. After all, if you've had an intense day of interactions, the last thing you may want or need is to go over things one more time.

But there's a third way to communicate at the end of the day—a way that's too often forgotten—and that's to ask her about her day. Does this have to become a daily pattern to be effective? Not necessarily, though if you are groaning at the thought of listening to how her day went, it may mean that this particular means of loving the love of your life is especially important for you to practice. For example, if you feel as if she drones on and on, that may be a simple matter that she doesn't feel listened to and is compensating by trying to get your attention. Practice asking about her day. Be consistent and listen to what she says. Then you should encounter no resentment when you come home on a particular night and communicate that you really do need some downtime to unwind after a tough day.

SHOW IT

Just because you know the rules of good listening doesn't mean you follow them! Ask her how her day was and then do the following: (a) really mean it, (b) make good eye contact, (c) don't interrupt her stories with stories of your own, editorial comments, or criticism and correction, (d) ask follow-up questions, and (e) don't rush her. Sound too simple? Go for it and give yourself a grade on each of the points above. Active listening isn't as easy as it sounds.

> Having someone who understands is a great blessing to ourselves. Being someone who understands is a great blessing to others.
>
> JANETTE OKE

PASS IT ON

When you pass the book to your wife, don't just leave it somewhere for her to find. Make eye contact, hand it to her, and ask, "Am I doing any better listening to you?" If she hasn't noticed yet, don't get defensive and explain or scold. Just, well, *listen* and smile, and when she's finished tell her, "I'm working on it!" ❤

Make Some Beautiful Music

*Speak to one another with psalms,
hymns and spiritual songs. Sing and
make music in your heart to the Lord.*

EPHESIANS 5:19 NIV

KNOW IT

Music is a sound the heart hears, because music encompasses and expresses every emotion: from anger to sorrow; from happiness to excitement; and yes, including love and affection. Have you ever noticed how, in some films, you feel moved by a combination of the action plus the soundtrack? If the music were removed, you might not feel as strong a connection to the characters and plot. In much the same way, music can capture the emotion behind the experiences in our own lives and express those emotions to others.

Music also has a unique way of bringing up old memories. What artists were you listening to when you realized you were in love with the love of your life? Is there a song you as a couple think of as "our song"?

Of course, the format of music has probably changed to keep up with the digital age since you were dating. One benefit of those advances is how easy it is to create your own custom album.

SHOW IT

If you don't already have a music download account, get online and set one up now. Then go through the searches and find songs that you enjoy as a couple and, most of all, that express how you feel about her. For a little over one buck per song, download an "I love you" album. If she has an iPod or other MP3 player, load it as a named album there. Otherwise, burn it on a CD. Then use an online CD "i-card" service, upload a picture, write a quick love note, and present it to her as a surprise.

Music is what feelings sound like.

AUTHOR UNKNOWN

PASS IT ON

If you can, find an old CD, cassette tape, or vinyl album—something you used to listen to when you and your wife were dating. Tag it with a note that says, "Remember this?" and leave it with the book for your wife to find. ❤

Take a Walk

*For bodily exercise profits
a little, but godliness is profitable
for all things, having promise of the life
that now is and of that which is to come.*

1 TIMOTHY 4:8

KNOW IT

Social scientists at the University of Maryland, Baltimore, identified a number of traits, qualities, and habits of healthy marriages, and high on the list was engaging in healthy physical activities together. Does that mean you have to go to the YMCA together every morning? Family scheduling and different workout routines and needs might make that impossible, but you can still incorporate some form of physical activity together as a mutual interest and shared time to talk and just be together.

In fact, taking an evening or morning walk together a couple times a week might enhance other ways and opportunities to express love to the love of your life—like holding hands, exploring new neighborhoods or parks, and knowing you can count on and look forward to that time together. But don't underestimate the individual health benefits of a moderate or intensely paced walk. Studies have noted benefits ranging from slowing down the aging process and adding healthy years to one's life, to improving one's general outlook on life and emotional health. Besides, feeling better can lead to expressing love better—both in the short term and long term of your marriage.

SHOW IT

This one is simple. Help her clean up the dishes after dinner and tell her to go put on her athletic shoes. Walk quickly by the television set. Leave the iPods, even if they are matching, at home. Don't slow down or get distracted. Grab her by the hand and head out the door for a thirty-minute walk. You do have time to do something healthy for her and for yourself—and, at the same time, show love to the love of your life. Now comes the hard part. Can you make this a regular part of your normal week? Two days a week? Three days a week? Don't sweat the number—but do sweat together!

> A fellow ought to save a few of the long evenings he spends with his girl till after they're married.
>
> KIN HUBBARD

PASS IT ON

If your budget can handle it, go out and buy her a new pair of walking or running shoes. She may take them back to swap for a better fit or a color she likes more, but it's the thought that counts. Put the book in the box with the shoes so she knows it's her turn when she gets her new shoes! ❤

Get Things Cookin'

Through love serve one another.
GALATIANS 5:13

KNOW IT

Maybe your wife does all the cooking in your house—or maybe you do. Or maybe you share the responsibility. Whoever cooks the meals, whatever culture or background you come from, and however much money you have to spend on meals, you know that food is an important aspect of your family's life and a powerful way to express your feelings for someone.

For one thing, sharing food together is an act of intimacy and friendship. There's something about sitting at a table together that strengthens a relationship. Is it any wonder that statistics show that kids who regularly eat dinner with Mom and Dad are better students and generally healthier emotionally and physically?

For another thing, serving food to someone is an act of love and nurturing. There's nothing like a good meal after a hard day, especially when it's prepared for you as an expression of love and care. So what better way to show your wife you love her than to fix her something wonderful to eat?

SHOW IT

Make dinner plans with your wife one night this week—but don't tell her where you're going. Choose a recipe, and pick up the ingredients. Then treat her to a home-cooked meal right in your own dining room. Make it something she likes, something that's a treat for both of you and gives you a chance to put your creativity to work. But if your culinary skills aren't so sharp, don't worry. Many tasty dishes score low on the difficulty range, and you can probably find a book of fun, easy recipes at your bookstore or library. Besides, the thought and effort you put into the meal will mean more to your wife than how good it tastes.

> ## Gestures, in love, are incomparably more attractive, effective, and valuable than words.
>
> FRANCOIS RABELAIS

PASS IT ON

Buy a simple kitchen gadget—an egg timer, a new whisk, a lemon zester, anything your wife might enjoy having—and place it with the book on your kitchen counter. ❤

Chick Flicks
Rule

*Each of us should please his
neighbor for his good, to build him up.*

ROMANS 15:2 NIV

KNOW IT

On the list of top-grossing movies of all time, the final installment of Peter Jackson's *Lord of the Rings* trilogy ranks high, as do various *Harry Potter* films. But the number one spot? It goes to *Titanic*. Somehow that movie combined action and romance into a worldwide crowd-pleaser.

Not such a big fan of the romance genre? They say that understanding Jane Austen's *Pride and Prejudice* is the key to understanding a woman's heart. Maybe seeing Colin Firth in a ruffled shirt doesn't get your romantic juices flowing. But those romantic movies have a way of adding a little romance to any evening, and you know they get your wife's attention.

It's true that some movies can set up unfair expectations or present an unrealistic, fairy-tale view of love. But watching a romantic movie your wife enjoys can help you see what she most longs for in her relationship with you. And if you take the time to watch one with her, there's a good chance you'll get *her* romantic juices flowing.

SHOW IT

Pick out a romance movie your wife likes, maybe one you own, maybe one you can rent that you know she loves, and invite her to watch it with you. Without complaining—and try to enjoy a romantic movie night together. You just might find that Colin Firth has a few tricks up his sleeve after all.

> Without expectation, do something for love itself,
> not for what you may receive.
>
> MOTHER TERESA

PASS IT ON

If your budget allows, pick up a DVD of a romantic movie your wife enjoys and leave it with the book for her to find. You might attach a note that says, "You're my favorite leading lady!" 💜

Put It
Differently

*Let love and faithfulness never
leave you; bind them around your neck,
write them on the tablet of your heart.*

KNOW IT

For better or worse... In sickness and in health... To love, honor, and cherish... We make important promises on our wedding day. We not only pledge our faithfulness and love; we vow that we will keep on loving and keep on being faithful years from now.

Even in the excitement of the day, with the cake and the limo and the throwing of the bouquet, what you and your wife want most is to know that those vows were said sincerely. That you not only love and like her, but that you're deeply committed to her and will stay with her until your dying day.

Marriage is a marathon, not a sprint. Love must be nurtured and maintained over time, and each day matters. And what will make your wife happiest and most secure in your marriage today is knowing that you are still as committed to loving her as you were the day you got married.

SHOW IT

Do you have a copy of your wedding vows? If so, get it out and read them over. If not, go over them in your memory. Then get out paper and pen and write your wife a letter of commitment. Put your vows in your own words. Leave them on her pillow one morning or make time to read it to her out loud.

One of the great illusions of our time is that love is self-sustaining. It is not. Love must be fed and nurtured, constantly renewed. That demands ingenuity and consideration, but first and foremost, it demands time.

DAVID MACE

PASS IT ON

If you two saved one of your wedding invitations, get it out and leave it with the book with a sticky note that says, "Best day of my life!" If you don't have an invitation—and for a thousand-point romantic bonus—make a pretend one on your computer or by hand that includes the date of your wedding as well as your promises for the future. ❤

Count Your Blessings

He who finds a wife finds a good thing,
And obtains favor from the LORD.

PROVERBS 18:22 NIV

KNOW IT

Dr. Steven Toepfer, an assistant professor at Kent State University, conducted a study among his students to assess the effect of gratitude and expressive writing on a person's level of happiness. He found that as his students wrote letters of appreciation to significant people in their lives, they grew happier, more grateful, and more satisfied with their lives.

Gratitude has a profound impact on how we view and deal with every event in our lives, from the smallest to the largest. When we are aware of our blessings, we feel better about our circumstances. Dr. Toepfer's findings, then, make a lot of sense. Maybe developing a sense of gratitude and happiness with our lives starts by telling the ones we love why we love and appreciate them.

Telling your wife that you consider her a blessing—and why—just might quicken your love and appreciation for her. It will certainly quicken her love and appreciation for you.

SHOW IT

Make a list of all the reasons you are blessed to be married to your wife. Then let her know. Write her a note titled "Here's What You Do That Blesses Me"—or just sit her down and read her your list. There's a good chance that after you share your list, the two of you will feel happier and more content with your life together and more hopeful about your future.

> Adam enthusiastically received Eve because he knew she was from God. Adam's faith in God enabled him to receive Eve as God's perfect provision for him.
>
> DENNIS RAINEY

PASS IT ON

Place the book beside her Bible with a sticky note that says Proverbs 18:22. ❤

Queen of the Road

The LORD shall preserve your going out and your coming in from this time forth, and even forevermore.

PSALM 121:8

KNOW IT

Author Gary Chapman identifies five love languages at work in marriages: words of affirmation, quality time, gifts, physical touch, and acts of service. Particularly if you or your wife communicate love primarily through acts of service, a simple everyday chore—walking the dog, doing the dishes, mowing the lawn—can become a powerful act of love. Especially when that chore is performed to the hilt and treated as though it were a special occasion.

Your wife probably spends a sizable chunk of time in the car every day. So one loving act of service—one she's sure to notice—might be to make her ride smoother. Go all out in doing a few car-maintenance chores, and she'll feel like she has the best car on the road as well as the best husband in town.

SHOW IT

Show your wife how much you care by waiting until she's not looking and carjacking her car, then taking the time to do all the maintenance items you can think of, both big and small. You could change the oil, rotate the tires, wash and wax it, detail the inside, change the air freshener, restock the coins for tolls. By showering her car with affection—and you know you want to anyway—you'll be showing her how much you care for her too.

The great acts of love are done by those who are habitually performing small acts of kindness.

AUTHOR UNKNOWN

PASS IT ON

Find one small, car-related gift, like a tire gauge or a map, and leave it with the book on the front seat of your wife's car. ❤

Photo
Collage

I remember the days of long ago;
I meditate on all your works
and consider what your hands have done.

PSALM 143:5 NIV

KNOW IT

If there's one key to your wife's heart, one thing that says you love her more clearly than anything else, it's a big gesture. You know this. You know the importance of flowers and surprises. But maybe you have a hard time thinking up meaningful gestures. We're here to help.

In addition to splashy displays of love, there's something else your wife loves: your family. With this activity, you'll tie the two things together and show your affection for both your wife and the family you have together. And that is a very quick route to her heart.

SHOW IT

If you're like many families in the digital age, you have metric tons of pictures lying around in paper sleeves or in digital form on your computer. Browse through them and pick out some favorites. You'll need quite a few, so shoot for sixty to one hundred. Look for shots that show all of you together and represent especially fun times for you.

Collect the ones you like and get them printed out if needed. Then, when your wife is out or busy, arrange them on your (made) bed. Spell out "I love you" or another message, or arrange them in a heart. Annotate the photos with sticky notes that say things like, "This was my favorite moment of that vacation," or "I love it when Jackson cracks up like that." You could even make a trail of photos and notes leading her from the front door to your room to witness your artwork.

When she does see your bed-canvas, she'll want to take one more picture and keep it forever.

Photography is a way of feeling, of touching, of loving. What you have caught on film is captured forever... It remembers little things, long after you have forgotten everything.

AARON SISKIND

PASS IT ON

Buy a small photo album and leave it with the book for your wife to find. Include a note that says, "Here's to the future!" ❤

Cut the Criticism

Let all bitterness,
wrath, anger, clamor,
and evil speaking be put
away from you, with all malice.
And be kind to one another,
tenderhearted, forgiving one another,
even as God in Christ forgave you.

EPHESIANS 4:31–32

KNOW IT

Words matter. They really do. As the biblical proverb puts it, "Pleasant words are like a honeycomb, sweetness to the soul and health to the bones" (Proverbs 16:24).

Maybe you don't speak harshly and critically to your wife very often. But if you've ever said something belittling or dismissed an idea of hers with a scoff and a roll of your eyes, there's a good chance she remembers it—and where the two of you were, and what you were wearing, and what she had to eat that day. And it probably didn't make her feel very good.

Marriages thrive in an atmosphere of genuine acceptance. So you'll help your marriage immensely by making an effort to speak helpfully in your home. Make the positive outweigh the negative, encourage her rather than put her down, model kind words for your kids, and you'll reap abundant rewards in your marriage.

SHOW IT

Set a goal to go the entire week without saying anything critical to your wife. If you have a conflict to resolve, do so; but try to keep your tone kind and avoid attacking your wife as a person. While you're stripping your speech of negative talk, replace it with positive words. Say thank you for little things; express appreciation for a job well done. This isn't an exercise in flattery. It is an attempt to look for the good in your wife and to make your relationship an environment of encouragement and respect.

When we really love others, we accept them as they are. We make our love visible through little acts of kindness, shared activities, words of praise and thanks, and our willingness to get along with them.

EDWARD E. FORD

PASS IT ON

Leave the book with some sweet treat—candy or a cookie from the grocery store deli—as a reminder of how sweet a few kind words can be. ❤

Love Your In-Laws

Therefore a man shall leave his father and mother and be joined to his wife, and they shall become one flesh.

GENESIS 2:24

KNOW IT

Right next to the biblical account of creation, we have the world's first marriage. When God "joins together" Adam and Eve, he tells them that they are to leave their families and "cleave" to each other. So loving the love of your life might mean you need to evaluate your relationship with your own parents and family. Who comes first? Her or them? Once that question is answered in your heart, then you can move on to enhancing your relationship with your in-laws.

You may be blessed with a wonderful relationship with your wife's parents and family, or you may struggle with unfair judgments and conflict that's not of your making. Whatever the condition of your relationship with your in-laws, you can show your wife how much you care about her by being respectful and warm to the people who brought her into the world. If she has a strained relationship with her parents, who knows, maybe you can create an environment where reconciliation and peace can flourish.

SHOW IT

Call your in-laws this week to catch up with what's going on with them and to let them know what's happening in your family. A simple, casual conversation that begins with your taking the initiative speaks volumes about how much you care for their daughter, you have made her family a priority. But in the next conversation, end with a thank you: thank them for their wonderful daughter and let them know how much you love your wife. She will hear about it sometime in the near future! Oh, and if you have tended to criticize your in-laws, this is a good moment to turn that pattern around and begin expressing sincere respect and appreciation.

Constant kindness can accomplish much.

ALBERT SCHWEITZER

PASS IT ON

Find a childhood picture of your wife. Tuck it in the front of her side of the book. Add a note that says, "Your parents sure knew how to make cute kids!" ❤

Whisper a Prayer

*We give thanks to the God
and Father of our Lord Jesus
Christ, praying always for you.*

COLOSSIANS 1:3 NIV

KNOW IT

Does prayer have an effect on our physical health? Can we measurably improve physical condition by intercessory prayer? Many researchers have endeavored to find out, with mixed results. And you probably know a lot of people who have anecdotal evidence about the power of prayer.

Of course, many will argue that it's our faith that makes a difference, that if we believe in prayer, our belief will better our health or change our situation. And maybe that's true in a way. After all, Jesus himself said to the woman with the issue of blood, "Your faith has healed you" (Matthew 9:22 NIV). When we reach out to God in faith, we often experience him in powerful ways. And when we know someone is reaching out to God on our behalf, we find our hopes lifted and our souls comforted.

Maybe that's why praying for someone—and letting her know you're doing so—is such a powerful act of love. For one thing, asking God to protect and guide your wife is the best thing you can do for her. For another, it shows her that you care about her deeply.

SHOW IT

Make the commitment to pray for your wife every day for the next week. Ask God to lead her, strengthen her, and give her joy. It might help you to tie your prayer commitment to some other part of your daily routine— your regular prayers, driving to work, or picking up the kids from activities. Don't be surprised if this habit extends past that initial week or if you end up praying for your wife more often than once a day. And don't be surprised if God works in your own heart in mighty ways.

If we truly love people, we will desire for them
far more than it is within our power to give them,
and this will lead us to prayer. Intercession
is a way of loving others.

RICHARD J. FOSTER

PASS IT ON

When you hand this book back to your wife, give her a hug and say, "I just
wanted to let you know I've been praying for you. I hope God is doing some
amazing things in your life." ❤

Take Her on a Date

Husbands, love your wives,
just as Christ also loved the
church and gave Himself for her.

EPHESIANS 5:25

KNOW IT

His doctorate wasn't in marriage and family relationships. It was in theology. Even so, the old professor had a few wise words about keeping a marriage going. "You want to know the secret to keeping the romance alive after you get married?" he asked his classes more than once, raising a finger for emphasis. "Keep dating."

It's amazing how rushed and harried we feel about life—particularly once we have children. With so much to get done every day and what seems like a shrinking amount of free time, we barely have a minute to pause for conversation with our family. And before long, we realize it's been quite awhile since we spent some time alone with the love of our life.

But time is one of the most important currencies of love. Investing some time in your relationship with your wife will show her that you value her. And when you put forth a little extra effort to make her feel special and cared for—flowers, maybe tickets to an event she wants to attend—your relationship will blossom.

SHOW IT

This weekend, arrange for a babysitter and take your wife out on an old-fashioned date: dinner, movie, coffee or ice cream, the works. Tell her to dress up, and you do the same. And don't forget the most important thing: have fun. Mentally lay aside your obligations and responsibilities, and look at this activity not as a task, but as a chance to act like a teenager with the love of your life.

There is a time for risky love. There is a time for extravagant gestures. There is a time to pour out your affections on the one you love. And when the time comes—seize it, don't miss it.

MAX LUCADO

PASS IT ON

Attach your ticket stubs or program—or some other memento from your date night—to a note thanking her for being such a great date. Place the note inside the book and pass it on to her. ❤

Spend Time with Your Kids

And you, fathers, do not provoke your children to wrath, but bring them up in the training and admonition of the Lord.

EPHESIANS 6:4

KNOW IT

The statistics are well known, well documented, and very clear: kids with loving, involved fathers are much more likely to excel academically and socially, and they are much less likely to get involved in risky behaviors like drugs and crime.

It's been said that if you want to do what's right by your kids, love their mother. The converse is also true: if you want to show love to your wife, love her kids—both the ones you have together and children she might have from a previous relationship. Loving your kids not only has an important impact on them—and you. It also demonstrates love to your wife.

Showing kids love is pretty simple; many of the same principles of loving your wife also apply to loving your kids. Spend time with them. Make an effort to know them and listen to them. Even if you have a rocky relationship with a surly teen or two, a little effort can go a long way—and provide them with a precious dose of love and attention they desperately need. And maybe, through the course of this book, you're finding out that sometimes the practice of love makes feelings of love flow a little more freely.

SHOW IT

Take each one of your kids out on a date. Take a little time for just the two of you—an afternoon in the park, a walk through the neighborhood, a trip to the ice cream place. If you have a big family, this one might be tricky to fit in your schedule, but try. Never underestimate the value of this time. It means more to your kids than you can imagine. And rest assured that it will put a smile on your wife's face as well.

Sharing time together is a precious gift of love
and trust that each family member gives to the
others. A strong sense of family unity, belonging,
and warmth doesn't just happen. It is nurtured and
grown over time, just as a lovely garden flourishes
in the hands of a caring, diligent gardener.

RICHARD PATTERSON JR.

PASS IT ON

Find a family photo and write on the back of it, "I love you guys so much."
Insert it in the front cover of the book and pass it on. ❤

Say It with Flowers

A bundle of myrrh is my beloved to me.
SONG OF SOLOMON 1:13

KNOW IT

You've probably given your wife a few bouquets of flowers during your tenure as a husband. Flowers have been used for centuries—millennia, probably—in celebrations and ceremonies and as gifts to express the giver's feelings. Today we use them to say "Congratulations," "I love you," and, of course, "I'm sorry."

You might not realize it, but most of the flowers at your florist's shop have very old, traditional meanings and long ago were used to say something specific. Red roses symbolize love and desire, while yellow roses symbolize friendship. Magnolia flowers represent dignity and beauty, while irises can symbolize faith, wisdom, and valor. And, depending on their color, carnations can have all sorts of meanings—some of which aren't very nice!

So while a gift of flowers might seem perfunctory and uncreative on some occasions, with a little thought—and as a spontaneous gesture—they might be a much-appreciated way to say, "I love you."

SHOW IT

Send your wife a surprise floral arrangement at work or at home. But do a little research first (try typing "flower meanings" into a search engine) to give a gift with meaning. That way, when she gushes over how pretty they are, you can tell her, "They're gladiolus. They represent strength of character, which is one thing I love about you" or "Pink and white roses together mean 'I will always love you.'" Put a little extra thought into this bouquet, and it will be one she never forgets.

> Flowers leave some of their fragrance
> in the hand that bestows them.
>
> CHINESE PROVERB

PASS IT ON

Pair the book with one more solitary flower and leave it on your wife's pillow.

Solicit Her Opinion

Take delight in honoring each other.
ROMANS 12:10 NLT

KNOW IT

No-Brainer Marriage Principle #208: You will not always agree. It's how you handle your disagreements that makes your marriage successful or unsuccessful.

Marriage researcher John Gottman has found that the predictors of divorce or marriage success might not be what everyone expected. Anger, for example, is not an evil in and of itself; only when it's mishandled or expressed with contempt does it become toxic to a marriage. And what does seem to indicate stability in a marriage is a partnership mentality and a willingness to accept each other's suggestions—specifically shown in a husband's ability to be influenced by his wife.

Okay, don't freak out. No one is asking you to be a kept man or to mindlessly repeat, "Yes, dear" all the livelong day. This principle is mostly about giving your wife's thoughts and opinions the consideration and concern you'd like her to show yours.

Of course, in order to accept each other's suggestions and opinions, you have to know what they are. As tempting as it may be to take a "me first" approach here and make sure your wife knows—and takes seriously—your opinion on every item that affects you as a couple, press the pause button on that impulse. You want your ideas heard, and you want to take a leadership role in your family, but you need to be willing to hear your wife's ideas too. Besides, when you take the initiative to listen respectfully to your partner's ideas, you'll make it easier for her to do the same for you.

So make the first move by soliciting and listening to her opinion on something that matters to both of you.

SHOW IT

Is there a pressing issue in your family's life right now? When the two of you have some time to talk, ask her what she thinks about that burning issue. If you tend to make decisions without asking her, she might be taken aback and unsure of how to express herself. Give her time to put her words together.

Even if you disagree, take the time to listen and ask her why she thinks what she does. It's not against the rules to share your own thoughts, and you probably won't decide anything tonight. But the importance of this exercise is to show respect and consideration for your wife's opinion.

> Every successful marriage requires necessary losses. For starters, marriage means coming to terms with new limits on one's independence.
>
> LES AND LESLIE PARROTT

PASS IT ON

Place the book inside your wife's purse with a note expressing thanks that she's your teammate. ❤

Read Out Loud from a Book of Poetry

Pleasant words are like a honeycomb,
sweetness to the soul and health to the bones.

PROVERBS 16:24

KNOW IT

It was Lord Byron who wrote:

> She walks in beauty, like the night
> Of cloudless climes and starry skies,
> And all that's best of dark and bright
> Meets in her aspect and her eyes.

That poem, written in 1814, has a very long history of melting women's hearts.

Maybe you don't think of yourself as the most romantic, poetic guy (and maybe your wife wears jeans quite a bit more often than Victorian dresses). Or maybe you have a fondness and appreciation for clever and beautiful language. Either way, spend a little time with the Romantic poets this week. You might find that they knew a thing or two about women—and even that their poems express your feelings better than you could on your own. You might also find that those old poets left you with a great way to romance your wife.

Lord Byron led a passionate life (admittedly, sometimes excessively so) that included many romances and a stint in the military. Pursuing your wife with that kind of passion and fire is a wonderful way to love the love of your life.

SHOW IT

Go to the library and find a collection of poetry—the kind you probably had to read in high school. Look for Longfellow, Tennyson, Whittier,

Shakespeare, and our old friend Lord Byron. Pick a few poems that speak to you. Then one evening as you and your wife are heading for bed, cap off your night with a little poetry reading. This is probably an out-of-the-ordinary occurrence for the two of you, so she'll be surprised. And you might feel a little embarrassed. But cast off a few inhibitions and speak beautiful words to your wife. And your evening will get a whole lot more romantic.

> ## My heart is ever at your service.
>
> WILLIAM SHAKESPEARE

PASS IT ON

Write out one of your favorite poems, one that best expresses how you feel about your wife. Leave it with the book on her pillow. ♥

Go for a Drive

You have put gladness in my heart,
more than in the season that their
grain and wine increased.

PSALM 4:7

KNOW IT

Researchers at DePauw University conducted an unusual study. They studied college yearbook photos and rated each person's smile on an intensity scale of one to ten. They found that the people with the most intense smiles were still married years later; those with weaker smiles showed a higher rate of divorce. It appears that youthful happiness might be an indicator of marital happiness.

In any case, it doesn't take a rocket scientist to figure out that happy marriages are . . . well . . . happy marriages. Cultivating a sense of fun and levity is bound to make your marriage feel less like work and more like the carefree closeness you both desire deep down. Plus, a focus on fun is bound to keep up the feeling of happiness and anticipation you felt when you were dating. And that surely never hurt a marriage.

So maybe a youthful activity is in order. Doing something you did as kids will drain all the seriousness—and maybe even some of the stress—out of your week. And it just might strike a spark of high-school romance between you and your wife.

SHOW IT

One evening this week, take your wife out on a scenic drive to look at the moon. You might have to do some sleuthing together to find the perfect spot, or you might have a place you used to go to as kids. Wherever you go, cast off your responsibilities and try to reconnect with the energy you had as teenagers. A scenic drive might be just what you need to liven up your week.

To get the full value of joy you must
have someone to divide it with.

MARK TWAIN

PASS IT ON

Leave the book on her car dashboard to find the next morning. ❤

Take a Class Together

*A wise man will hear
and increase learning,
and a man of understanding
will attain wise counsel.*

PROVERBS 1:5

KNOW IT

When Bob and Jeanne faced an empty nest for the first time, they went through a brief period of bewilderment. Their schedules had revolved around their kids' activities for so long. What would they do now that they didn't have the kids to bring them together? After much discussion, they decided to landscape their backyard just as they'd always meant to. They took a horticulture class at the local university extension and ended up having more fun together than they ever had before. And within the year, they had a pretty nice lawn to show for it to boot.

Learning something new is always a growth experience, sometimes a grueling one. And when you share that experience with someone else, it bonds you together in a unique way. You get to see new sides of her as you explore the subject matter, and you learn to depend on each other's strengths. For these reasons, taking a class with your wife is an investment in her, in yourself, and in your life together.

If nothing else, going to class and doing assignments together will give you lots of time to spend with each other. And according to Ted Futris, a family life specialist with Ohio State University, sharing experiences and spending unforced time together is a big indicator of a healthy marriage.

A lengthy, demanding class might involve more time and money than you can invest right now. But even a day class or seminar of interest to both of you will give you a chance to stretch your brains and grow your marriage.

SHOW IT

Put your thinking cap on and do a little research into classes in your area. Public libraries are a great place to start, and remember that many colleges will allow you to audit courses. You might also find an interesting class or seminar at your home church or another local congregation.

The class you choose can be practical and useful or purely for fun. Bring home the literature and ask your wife if she would be interested. The truth is that even if she's not so into the idea, she'll be touched by your offer.

> Develop a passion for learning.
> If you do, you will never cease to grow.
>
> ANTHONY J. D'ANGELO

PASS IT ON

Look for a nonfiction book at the library that might interest your wife. Maybe she's interested in history or health or spiritual growth. Tuck this book inside the library book and attach a note that says, "Thought this might interest you." Leave both books somewhere she's sure to notice them. ❤

Your Turn

Love never fails.

1 CORINTHIANS 13:8

On the other side of this page is one final activity, one you'll share with your wife. But before you turn the page, pause for a minute. Think back on the previous weeks or months and the activities you've completed. And ask yourself a few questions:

💜 Which activity in this book received the most enthusiastic response from your wife?

💜 Which one did you enjoy most as the giver, and which as the receiver?

💜 In what ways do you think your efforts to practice loving your wife have paid off in your marriage?

Now it's your turn. With the answers to the above questions in mind, think up one last activity, one more way of showing love to your spouse. Make it something specific to her, her desires and soft spots, her tastes, and something meaningful to you as well.

If you've learned anything through the course of this book, we hope it's that love put into words and actions can grow stronger each day. Sometimes our efforts might be and feel awkward; and sometimes we miss the mark a little. But when we make loving our spouse a priority, our efforts pay off.

work is
that needs sor
of our relationsh
I think one ar

What do we do together that you
most enjoy?

Something I learned from
working through this book
with you is . . .

houghts honestly in answering each
question. You've spent several weeks
nurturing the love and trust in your
relationship. Now it's time to flex those
muscles and evaluate both where you are
s a couple and where you want to go.

Meet in

What do I do that makes
you feel loved? Is there
anything I do that makes
you feel unloved?

Start
Here

nething you
ve done for me
ently that really
owed me how
ich you love me is . . .

Something I really like to do to show
you how much I love you is . . .

Loving the Love of Your Life

of Your Life

Show Him How Much You Really Care

(And See What Happens Next!)

Loving the Love of Your Life

Copyright © 2009 Mark Gilroy Creative, LLC

Published in Nashville, Tennessee, by Thomas Nelson®
Thomas Nelson® is a registered trademark of Thomas Nelson, Inc.

Unless otherwise indicated, Scriptures are taken from The Holy Bible,
New King James Version © 1979, 1980, 1987, 1988, 1991,
by Thomas Nelson, Inc., Publishers.

Other Scripture references are taken from the HOLY BIBLE, NEW INTERNATIONAL
VERSION® (NIV). Copyright © 1973, 1978, 1984 International Bible Society.
Used by permission of Zondervan. All rights reserved; and Holy Bible, New Living
Translation (NLT) © 1996. Used by permission of Tyndale House
Publishers, Inc., Wheaton, Ill. All rights reserved.

Thomas Nelson, Inc. titles may be purchased in bulk for educational,
business, fund-raising, or sales promotional use. For information,
please e-mail SpecialMarkets@ThomasNelson.com.

Project Editor: Mark Gilroy Creative, LLC

Designed by ThinkpenDesign, Inc., www.thinkpendesign.com

ISBN-13: 978-1-4041-8764-1

Printed and bound in the United States of America

www.thomasnelson.com

Table of Contents

Introduction
For Wives Only
(No peeking, guys.)

When you look around at your friends' and family's marriages and at your own, you realize that marriages are as different as the people in them. But whether a couple is blissfully happy or on the brink of disaster, there's one thing every marriage has in common: room for improvement. Love must be nurtured if it's going to thrive and grow—every single day.

That's where this book comes in. Because love isn't really a feeling as much as a practice. And by practicing love, you enable the love-feelings to grow deeper. Along the way, mutual trust and respect are built up; resentments crumble and give way to forgiveness; and a climate of love and appreciation begins to form—all markers of a happy and stable marriage. We hope to give you tools and ideas for loving the love of your life practically and actively, getting you on the road to the marriage you long for.

As you get started, here are some simple guidelines:

1. If you're going through it with your husband, take turns reading and doing the activities in each chapter, using your own creativity to add to or modify an activity any way you'd

like. Read the "Know It" section, take the action step in the "Show It" section, then give the book back to your husband by following the instructions in the "Pass It On" section. Now it's his turn. Don't pick up the book again until he passes it back to you. And no flipping the book over and peeking at activities he might have planned for you.

2. If you're working through this book on your own, don't lose heart—one person's efforts in a marriage can go a long, long way, even if they're not immediately reciprocated.

3. Go for it. Some of these activities might seem a little goofy, maybe a little high-school. But try to let go of your mundane adult seriousness and just go for it! A little goofiness might be just what you need to rekindle that youthful spark you felt when you were dating.

4. There's one more guideline for using this book, and it's critical: no peeking! Okay, that's been mentioned, but we know it's tempting. Those blue pages are just a short finger-walk away from your side of the book, and wouldn't it be nice to know what he is cooking up? But you'll appreciate your husband's activities better if you receive them without expectation. Let yourself be surprised, and let your husband surprise you.

So turn the page to the first chapter and settle down in your chair to read and make plans for showing the one you love that you love him. He won't know what hit him—and neither will your marriage. ❤

Lend Me an Ear

*My dear brothers, take note
of this: Everyone should be quick
to listen, slow to speak and
slow to become angry.*

JAMES 1:19 NIV

KNOW IT

We spend much of our waking time in communication with others. Of that time, we spend about 9 percent writing, 16 percent reading, 30 percent speaking, and 45 percent listening. But sometimes we don't spend our listening time very well. We're busy and wish the other person would hurry up, or we find our minds drifting to our to-do list, or we're desperate to spill our own guts. We don't give our full focus to what the other person is saying.

But when we listen intently to someone, we show that person that we value him or her, and listening is a vital part of a marriage. When you're listening to your husband, you're showing love and respect for him, because you're showing him that what he says is important to you. That's crucial.

Maybe your guy isn't the type to open up easily and share his emotions. That's okay. For one thing, if you give him a little room by listening attentively, you might be surprised by what he ends up sharing. For another thing, even if all he's talking about is what's going on at work or what projects he has planned for the summer, your attention will be a priceless gift of love to him.

SHOW IT

Sometimes men don't feel much like talking, especially at the end of the day; his body language will let you know if he's not in the mood for conversation. But when the time is right, ask him a question, even if it's a simple one like "What did you do at work today?" Really listen to his answer. Use your body language to show that you're paying attention: turn your shoulders toward him and make good eye contact. Showing an interest in what he has to say is a great way to love the love of your life.

The first duty of love is to listen.

PAUL TILLICH

PASS IT ON

Return the book to your husband with a small package of those Valentine heart candies with messages printed on them. Or, if the candies are seasonally unavailable, make your own hearts out of construction paper, writing short messages that have special meaning for the two of you. 💜

Be a Sport

For physical training is of some value....
1 TIMOTHY 4:8 NIV

KNOW IT

Baseball great Rogers Hornsby once spoke about his superlative dedication to his sport: "People ask me what I do in winter when there's no baseball. I'll tell you what I do. I stare out the window and wait for spring."

Men and sports. They go together like stadium hot dogs and antacid tablets. It's not just that men (well, by and large, anyway) enjoy sports. It's that sports are deeply important to them. Why else would sports coverage so dominate their TV viewing?

There are probably a lot of reasons for this. Sports appeal to the warrior within and feed the sports fan's competitive drive. Watching sports on TV might bring back good memories about belonging to a team as a youth. And it gives men a chance to vicariously live out those competitive, blood-pumping, victorious experiences.

So why not show your guy you appreciate what's important and fun for him by encouraging his love of sports? Any sports-related gift will do the trick. Surprise tickets don't have to be for major league sports; tickets to a local college basketball or football game or a minor league baseball game will be fine. Or try a sport different from the usual, something like soccer or hockey. Whatever you choose, go to the game with him and have fun.

SHOW IT

Surprise your husband with tickets to a sporting event. Or, alternatively, plan a party for the big game night. Invite his friends. Serve hot wings, nachos, and his favorite beverages. As you're leaving the game or straightening up after the party, thank him for being such a good sport and tell him how much you appreciate his fun and competitive nature.

Sports is human life in microcosm.

HOWARD COSELL

PASS IT ON

Place the book inside his old baseball glove or alongside some other sports memento and leave it somewhere for him to find it. ❤

Reenact a Favorite Date

I remember the days of long ago;
I meditate on all your works
and consider what your hands have done.

PSALM 143:5 NIV

KNOW IT

The first date is an important part of every married couple's story. A reenactment of their parents' first date is what Hailey Mills (and Hailey Mills) used in an attempt to get Brian Keith and Maureen O'Hara back together in *The Parent Trap*. And many would-be fiancés reenact their first date with their significant other as they stage their marriage proposals. That kind of reminiscence is irresistibly romantic.

Remember when you first started dating your guy? The excitement that bordered on giddiness as you got ready for a date; the pleasure of getting to know him combined with the heady thrill of thinking this could really turn into something; and the simple fun of spending time together before you had so many shared responsibilities. Those were good days. And even though love grows deeper over time and surpasses that initial attraction, keeping those memories alive can help maintain the thrill you felt when you first met.

Maybe you have one especially great date in mind—maybe it was even the one when you knew the two of you had a future together. Particularly if you've been together a long time, that date is an important part of your life together. So refresh those memories and rekindle the romance. And you just might find that the two of you have just as much heat as when you first started dating.

SHOW IT

Re-create a favorite date in your mind; an old photo album might help refresh your memory. Then take your husband out for a nostalgic good time. If possible, go to the very same restaurant, shop, or park you went to

so long ago, or rent the same movie you watched together. At some point in the evening, tell him why that night meant so much to you and how proud you are of how far the two of you have come.

> Touching and talking and holding hands and gazing into one another's eyes and building memories are as important to partners in their mid-life years as to rambunctious twenty-year-olds.
>
> James Dobson

PASS IT ON

Find a photo of the two of you early on in your relationship. Insert it in the book with a note that says, "Remember this?" and leave it for him to find.

Get Something Cooking!

May the Lord make you
increase and abound in love
to one another and to all.

1 THESSALONIANS 3:12

KNOW IT

According to Nielsen, February 13 is the number-one day for candy and chocolate sales each year. And Valentine's week takes up more than 5 percent of all annual chocolate sales.

"The way to a man's heart is through his stomach"—how long have people been saying that? Maybe your man is a little more complex, and the way to his heart is a little more nuanced than mere gastronomic pleasure. Even so, he probably loves a special culinary treat as much as the next guy. And his mom's cookies probably still ring in his memory as gooey symbols of love.

Besides, think about it: nearly every special occasion, every celebration of love and connection, involves some form of dessert. Birthday cake on birthdays, fudge and sugar cookies at Christmas, chocolate-covered cherries at Valentine's Day—these serve as ample evidence of the affectionate power of sweets. So maybe it's true that nothing says lovin' like something from the oven.

SHOW IT

Block off a little time to make your husband a sweet treat. You might enlist the kids' help—they'll love messing up the kitchen, and your husband will appreciate their contribution to this loving gesture. If you're not a baker at heart, don't count yourself out: cake mixes can do amazing things.

For a bonus, do a little research by asking family members about your husband's favorite dessert as a kid, then creating it in your own kitchen. For an extra bonus, go absolutely all out in decorating the cookies, cakes, or brownies you make and write "I love you" in icing.

> The great acts of love are done by those who are habitually performing small acts of kindness.
>
> AUTHOR UNKNOWN

PASS IT ON

Pair the book with a Saran-wrapped cookie—homemade or store-bought—and leave them in your husband's briefcase or with his car keys. Include a note that says, "One for the road. I love you!"

Cut the Criticism

Let all bitterness,
wrath, anger, clamor,
and evil speaking be put
away from you, with all malice.
And be kind to one another,
tenderhearted, forgiving one another,
even as God in Christ forgave you.

EPHESIANS 4:31–32

KNOW IT

Words matter. They really do. Sometimes we get busy and stressed and stop paying attention to what is flying out of our mouths. But the people closest to us are hearing every word.

Maybe you don't think of yourself as one of "those" wives—harsh, critical, berating their husbands (or kids) almost constantly. But stop and think: Do you say mostly positive things to him? Do you build him up, or do you belittle him? Do you encourage, or do you criticize?

There might be deeper reasons why you think or speak harshly about your husband, reasons you shouldn't ignore. But in the meantime, you'll help your marriage immensely by making an effort to speak helpfully in your home. Little everyday words of affirmation will make your marriage thrive; they're like water to a houseplant. Speak positively, and you'll reap the rewards.

SHOW IT

Set a goal to go the entire week without saying anything critical toward your husband. If you have a conflict to resolve or emotions to express, do so; but try to keep your tone kind and avoid attacking your husband as a person. While you're stripping your speech of negative talk, replace it with positive words. Say "thank you" for little things; if he does a good job with something, say so. This isn't an exercise in sycophantic flattery. But it is an attempt to look for the good in your husband and make your life together a haven of encouragement and respect.

When you look for the good and
honorable in your mate, you will find it.
God instilled His glory into each of us.

GARY SMALLEY

PASS IT ON

This time, hand the book to your husband in person. As you do so, ask this important question: "Do you ever feel criticized by me?" Listen to his answer, and if he does express a wish for you to be more encouraging, let him know you'll try to do better in the future. 💜

Inspector
Gadget

The generous soul will be
made rich, and he who waters
will also be watered himself.

PROVERBS 11:25

KNOW IT

According to America's Consumer Electronics Association, female consumers have recently caught up with—and in some categories surpassed—their male counterparts when it comes to spending money on electronics.

But this statistic is a recent development. When it comes to gadgets, the guys have tended to edge women out as voracious consumers. Go to any electronics or car-stereo store, and you'll probably see lots of excited guys, and at least one woman shaking her head at another and saying, "Boys and their toys." High on the list of things men get excited about is a fancy gadget. Whether it's a top-of-the-line tool for the shop, a phone that does everything, or a massive home entertainment system, there is probably some electronic something that your husband has been drooling over.

You may not understand the appeal, and you may not be very interested in electronics yourself. But showing your husband that you appreciate and encourage his love for grown-up toys will also show him that you love and appreciate him.

SHOW IT

Do a little sleuthing to find out what technological tool your husband has been eyeing. Maybe it's the latest and greatest smart phone, or new speakers for his car, or some top-of-the-line fishing equipment. If it's in your budget to do so, buy it for him and present it as a special gift. And if he's the type to buy what he wants, try to beat him to this one.

Maybe the two of you can't really afford a big electronics splurge right

paperwork and say to your husband, "Let's save up slowly to buy you that phone you want."

> To love by freely giving is its own reward.
>
> GLORIA GAITHER

PASS IT ON

Leave the book in his sock drawer as a surprise for him to find. ❤

How Do I Love Thee?

*Therefore comfort each other and edify
one another, just as you also are doing.*

1 THESSALONIANS 5:11

KNOW IT

Remember that scene in *When Harry Met Sally* when Billy Crystal surprises Meg Ryan at a New Year's Eve party and launches into a speech about why he loves her? That speech—"I love it that it takes you an hour and a half to order a sandwich"—is a classic. Maybe what makes it so immortal is that we all want to be loved that way.

Part of being loved is being unconditionally accepted, flaws and all. But another part of being loved is simply being liked—being appreciated, admired, and enjoyed. If the man we love doesn't know what we admire in him, he is missing out on our love a little. So when we love someone, we ought to tell him just what we love about him.

Sometimes in the day to day we simply get too busy to express our affection verbally; we think some things go without saying. Or maybe expressing encouragement and admiration for your loved one feels awkward—it can be hard to find a way to bring it up in conversation naturally. But if you'll make an effort to affirm your husband, you'll nurture your own feelings of love for him, as well as his for you.

SHOW IT

Get out paper and a pen and write a kind of top-ten list for your husband, "My 10 Favorite Things About You." Maybe it's his kindness with the kids; maybe it's his sense of humor and the things he finds funny; maybe it's his fashion sense (or lack thereof) that melts your heart. Whatever it is, write it down. Then leave it on his pillow to let him know just what you love about him.

Now if you want to get really creative, use an online design program or dust off that calligraphy set you haven't used for years and turn this top-ten into a piece of art. Frame it so he always has a visible reminder of how much you respect and admire him.

> Affection is not much good unless it is expressed. Putting an emotion into words gives it a life and a reality that otherwise it doesn't have. Expressing confidence in a person's ability to accomplish something actually strengthens that ability.
>
> ARTHUR GORDON

PASS IT ON

Find a dry-erase marker and make a circle in the middle of the bathroom mirror, right where your husband's face will be the next time he steps up to the sink. Label the circle "My Favorite Guy." Then draw an arrow pointing down and leave the book there on the counter. ❤

A Pat on the Back

Your love is more delightful than wine.
SONG OF SOLOMON 1:2 NIV

KNOW IT

We all know hugs are nice. You almost can't turn your head without seeing the value of hugs extolled on a coffee mug or in a comic strip, with lines like "A hug is the shortest distance between friends." Your guy may not be the most comfortable hugger around; ooey-gooey displays of affection might not come naturally to him. But he probably appreciates—and needs—regular loving touches from you.

Physical contact is a human need, a key contributor to our overall mental and physical health. Researchers have long extolled such physiological benefits of meaningful touches as lowered blood pressure and elevated hemoglobin levels. It's suggested that all of us need eight to ten meaningful touches each day to maintain good health.

Your husband is no different. Some physical attention will make him feel attended to, cared about, and much less stressed. (Of course that other kind of physical attention matters too—and might have a similar effect.) When you take the time to give him a long back rub, or you sprinkle in some physical affection throughout the day, you just might watch his stress melt away—and you'll probably be the recipient of a big bear hug of gratitude.

SHOW IT

Tell your husband to sit down, relax, and take off his shoes, because it's time for a back rub. Take your time, don't watch the clock. Maybe put in a DVD you both enjoy or turn on some soothing music. Dig deep into the tension in his muscles. And let your fingers show him you love him.

> Everybody needs a hug.
> It changes your metabolism.
>
> LEO BUSCAGLIA

PASS IT ON

Pass the book back to your husband with a spontaneous hug and kiss and an encouraging word or two. ❤

Make Some Beautiful Music

Speak to one another with psalms,
hymns and spiritual songs. Sing and
make music in your heart to the Lord.

EPHESIANS 5:19 NIV

KNOW IT

Music is a sound the heart hears, because music encompasses and expresses every emotion: from anger to sorrow; from happiness to excitement; and, yes, including love and affection. Have you ever noticed how, in some films, you feel moved by a combination of the action plus the soundtrack? If the music were removed, you might not feel as strong a connection to the characters and plot. In much the same way, music can capture the emotion behind the experiences in our own lives and express those emotions to others.

Music also has a unique way of bringing up old memories. What artists were you listening to when you realized you were in love with the love of your life? Is there a song you as a couple think of as "our song"?

Of course, the format of music has probably changed to keep up with the digital age since you were dating. One benefit of those advances is how easy it is to create your own custom album.

SHOW IT

If you don't already have a music download account, get online and set one up now. Then go through the searches and find songs that you enjoy as a couple and, most of all, that express how you feel about your guy. For a little over one buck per song, download an "I love you" album. If he has an iPod or other MP3 player, load it as a named album there. Otherwise, burn it on a CD. Then use an online CD "i-card" service, upload a picture, write a quick love note, and present it to him as a surprise.

Music is what feelings sound like.

AUTHOR UNKNOWN

PASS IT ON

Leave the book on his car dashboard for him to find first thing in the morning. Now he can think of you when he's driving as he listens to your CD. ❤

The Lawn Mower

*I thank my God upon
every remembrance of you.*

PHILIPPIANS 1:3

KNOW IT

Many husbands aren't so much into housework. Let's just say they don't have the same relationship with cleanliness that their wives do. But many of those same hubbies do a lot of other things around the house, like maintain the cars and keep the garage tidy.

There are probably a few chores around your house that you hate doing. And among those, your husband probably does a few—take out the trash, wrestle the dog to give him his medicine, or mow the lawn.

Even if your husband thrives on yard work and lives to mow the lawn, he could probably use a few words of thanks for his hard work. Marriages thrive on a sense of teamwork and gratitude for each spouse's contributions; just as you need to feel appreciated, so does your mate. You can nurture mutual appreciation in your marriage by expressing gratitude for all your husband does. Because chances are, he does what he does just for you.

SHOW IT

When you know your husband will be mowing the lawn soon, find some sidewalk chalk and mark a trail on the concrete leading toward the lawn mower—through the garage, across the driveway to the shed, wherever you store your yard tools—using arrows, pictures, or messages like "You're getting closer!" When you reach the mower, write, "Thank you for all you do for us!" in big, cheerful letters on the surrounding concrete.

If the two of you live in an apartment and don't need to mow the lawn, or if you're the primary lawn care specialist in your family, look for another chore your husband does and show him your appreciation for that. If you

think hard about all he does around the house, you might be surprised at the opportunities you have to express gratitude.

> Be presidents of each other's fan clubs.
>
> TONY HEATH

PASS IT ON

If you can, find some small tool that will make your husband's chores easier—gloves, a hand tool for gardening, a new set of shop rags—and place it with the book in his work area. ❤

Whisper a Prayer

*We give thanks to the God
and Father of our Lord Jesus
Christ, praying always for you.*

COLOSSIANS 1:3 NIV

KNOW IT

Does prayer have an effect on our physical health? Can we measurably improve physical condition by intercessory prayer? Many researchers have endeavored to find out, with mixed results. And you probably know a lot of people who have anecdotal evidence about the power of prayer.

Of course, many will argue that it's our faith that makes a difference, that if we believe in prayer, our belief will better our health or change our situation. And maybe that's true in a way. After all, Jesus himself said to the woman with the issue of blood, "Your faith has healed you" (Matthew 9:22 NIV). When we reach out to God in faith, we often experience him in powerful ways. And when we know someone is reaching out to God on our behalf, we find our hopes lifted and our souls comforted.

Maybe that's why praying for someone—and letting him know you're doing so—is such a powerful act of love. For one thing, asking God to protect and guide him is the best thing you can do for him. For another, it shows him that you care about him deeply.

SHOW IT

Make the commitment to pray for your husband every day for the next week. Ask God to lead him, strengthen him, and give him joy. It might help you to tie your prayer commitment to some other part of your daily routine—your regular prayers, loading the dishwasher, or driving to pick up your kids from school. Don't be surprised if this habit extends past that initial week or if you end up praying for him more often than once a day. And don't be surprised if God works in your own heart in mighty ways.

> If we truly love people, we will desire for them far more than it is within our power to give them, and this will lead us to prayer. Intercession is a way of loving others.
>
> RICHARD J. FOSTER

PASS IT ON

When you hand this book back to your husband, give him a hug and say, "I just wanted to let you know I've been praying for you. I hope God is doing some amazing things in your life." ♥

Dinner in Bed

Through love serve one another.

GALATIANS 5:13

KNOW IT

Have your kids ever made you breakfast in bed? Even if the pancakes were unevenly cooked and the bacon a little too crispy, that was one meal you probably never forgot. Did you ever make breakfast in bed for your mom as a kid? She probably never forgot that meal either.

Food can be a powerful symbol of love and community. Is there anything better than being served a delicious meal and enjoying it slowly in the company of loved ones? Perhaps the only way to make a luxurious meal better would be to eat it in bed.

Breakfast in bed has been a longtime Mother's Day staple, an opportunity to pamper someone who does so much for you. Why not extend a similar gesture to your husband? A favorite meal served in the comfort of the bedroom will help him de-stress, give the two of you some uninterrupted time together, and show him how much you love him.

SHOW IT

Pick a night this week—and maybe it's best to choose one when the kids will be out of the house at activities—and plan a delicious dinner for your husband. Choose a meal he loves and pick up the drinks of his choice. Then assemble everything together, not at the dining room table, but in your room. Invite him in for a delicious dinner for two, and watch the expression on his face turn to awe and delight.

My heart is ever at your service.

WILLIAM SHAKESPEARE

PASS IT ON

Buy a gift card from one of your husband's favorite places to get snacks or coffee; it doesn't have to be for a large amount—just a token will do. Insert the card in the front cover of the book and pass it back to him.

Go to the Zoo

The LORD is good to all,
And His tender mercies
are over all His works.

PSALM 145:9 NIV

KNOW IT

There are around 240 zoos accredited by America's Association of Zoos and Aquariums. That means there's probably a quality zoo in your area.

Zoos make a fun date. You can leisurely walk around holding hands and pointing out the different animals. You can observe what your mate finds interesting, charming, or gross. You can discover fun facts about the animal kingdom together—did you know that African elephants can weigh up to 15,000 pounds?—and learning new things is always a kind of bonding experience.

More than anything, though, the zoo provides you with something priceless: time to be together. And according to Ted Futris, a family life specialist with Ohio State University, sharing experiences and spending unforced time together is a big indicator of a healthy marriage.

So what better way to love the love of your life than to invest in some time with him? Well, him and the polar bears.

SHOW IT

Get your calendars out and schedule a zoo date. Pack some lunches, slather on some sunscreen, and make your way to your local zoo. Make it a point to not hurry: see the exhibits you want, but don't pressure yourselves to get to everything. Make sure there's time for leisurely walks along the sidewalk.

If there's not a zoo in your area, or if a full day at the zoo is a little more time than you can spend, find a DVD of a segment from the Discovery Channel's *Planet Earth* series. Guys have really bought into adventure and wildlife shows, and this well-made nature documentary will be an educational good time for both of you.

Receive the world that God has given.
Go for a walk. Get wet. Dig the earth.

ARCHBISHOP ROWAN WILLIAMS

PASS IT ON

Find a stuffed animal—preferably something in the simian family. Pair it with a banana and the book and leave it on your husband's pillow with a note that says, "I go monkeys for you!" If that strikes you as a little too goofy, just go with a stuffed animal and a note thanking your husband for a good time. ♥

Just Fore You

*Let us not love with words or
tongue but with actions and in truth.*

1 JOHN 3:18 NIV

KNOW IT

In America, more than 20 million men and almost 6 million women play golf. For some, it is as relaxing as a walk in the park; for others, it is a networking tool; and for some, it is a frustrating activity that drives blood pressure higher than anything they hit off the tee.

Golf is a separate activity for many couples, even when husband and wife both play. Consider this activity together as a way of showing him how much you love him—whether or not he, or you, play golf.

SHOW IT

Keep this outing a surprise. If the love of your life is a big-time golfer, this might even be an opportunity to add a gift to the surprise. If he is a regular golfer, visit a pro shop or retail store and ask if they have drivers to loan for a hitting session. This will give him an opportunity to try some new equipment out.

Whether or not you get a couple loaners, take your husband to the golfing range. Buy three buckets of balls—two for him and one for you. Let him go first and then, if you're new to golf, have him teach you how to drive with the second bucket of balls. Then tell him to enjoy himself on the third bucket while you go get refreshments.

Good, bad, or ugly, have a blast. If this has no interest whatsoever to you—all the more reason to try it as a way of letting him know you love him.

When we really love others, we accept them as they
are. We make our love visible through little acts
of kindness, shared activities, words of praise and
thanks, and our willingness to get along with them.

EDWARD E. FORD

PASS IT ON

If your husband golfs, buy a new package of balls and use a string to tie
together the book and balls. If he doesn't golf, find another token gift to
include with the book. ❤

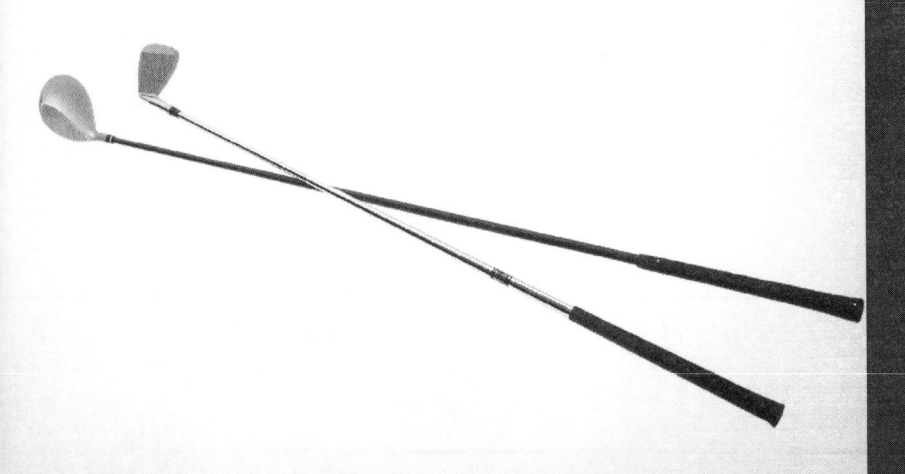

And Action!

Each of us should please his neighbor for his good, to build him up.

ROMANS 15:2 NIV

KNOW IT

On the list of top-grossing movies of all time, the final installment of Peter Jackson's *Lord of the Rings* trilogy ranks high, as do various *Harry Potter* films. But the number one spot? It goes to *Titanic*. Somehow that movie combined action and romance into a worldwide crowd-pleaser.

You've been there before. You're at the video store browsing through the new releases, and you see him reach for one of the cases and read the back of it. Groan. Another shoot-'em-up. You think, *Do I really want to spend this evening watching a series of car chases and explosions?* You look longingly at a romantic comedy.

Whatever you have in your hand when the two of you leave the video store—a rom-com, an action flick, or a compromise—you have just felt that familiar conflict of taste in movies. Maybe one way to show him you care about and appreciate his likes and tastes is to give one of his favorite movies a chance. It might help you discover why he likes them so much. Okay, maybe not. But it will show him that you care enough about him to fill his evening with his favorite entertainment.

SHOW IT

Go to the video store (whether online or brick-and-mortar is up to you) and pick out a movie you know he would enjoy, even—and maybe especially— if it's not quite up your own alley. Then suggest that you two watch it together. Take the initiative. No complaining—and no mocking! You might enjoy the film more than you think (Jason Bourne, for example, is a pretty compelling character). But even if you don't, you'll have made his evening—and shown him that you love him.

Small things, done in great love, bring joy and peace. To love, it is necessary to give. To give, it is necessary to be free from selfishness.

MOTHER TERESA

PASS IT ON

Print or clip from a magazine a photo of a tough character from a favorite action movie—the Terminator, perhaps, or Bruce Willis in *Die Hard*. Place it inside the book cover, sticking out a little so he'll notice it, along with a note that says, "You're my action hero!" Leave the book on his car seat before work in the morning. 💜

Take Him on a Picnic

He brought me to the banqueting house,
And his banner over me was love.

KNOW IT

Is there anything more romantic than a picnic? A checkered blanket, a basket full of food. It's the stuff of 1950s Kim Novak movies—i.e., 1955's *Picnic*, her breakout film co-starring William Holden.

You and your husband may not have been on too many picnics together, or you might have a memory or two of lunching and canoodling in the park. Either way, now is a great time for a romantic picnic lunch for two. Use it as an opportunity to enjoy some scenic views in your area. Or use it as a chance to put together some old-fashioned picnic foods—watermelon, deviled eggs, Jell-O salad, potato salad, macaroni salad . . . the options are endless. Of course, most importantly, use it as a chance to have a romantic afternoon.

SHOW IT

Plan an old-school picnic for you and your husband. Pick a location—your favorite park or one you haven't visited yet, or stop on a scenic drive. If the weather is uncooperative, even your living room floor can serve as a picnic grounds. If the two of you are outdoorsy types, or if only your husband is, you might consider planning a hike to your picnic location.

Next, plan a menu and pick up the ingredients. Cheese, crackers, olives, fruit, and lunch meats are all good picnic staples. If you have a picnic basket, so much the better, but a backpack will do fine for packing up the prepared goodies. Don't forget napkins, plates, and your favorite drinks. And to add to your afternoon, bring along a portable CD player for ambience. You might also consider other entertainment for the day—cards, Frisbees, maybe even a portable DVD player with a romantic movie queued up.

Whatever you do, make it a special day. Above all, enjoy some time with your guy.

Moments spent listening, talking, playing, and sharing together may be the most important times of all.

GLORIA GAITHER

PASS IT ON

Spread a picnic blanket out over your bed and leave the book on it with a note thanking him for a wonderful picnic lunch.

Tell the Story of How You Met

Kiss me and kiss me again,
for your love is sweeter than wine.
How fragrant your cologne; your
name is like its spreading fragrance.
No wonder all the young women love you!

SONG OF SOLOMON 1:2–4

KNOW IT

Some first-time-we-met stories are more exciting than others. Some involve wartime separation or freak, happenstance meetings. Others fall more along the lines of "We met through friends" or "We met on the Internet." Whatever your story is, telling it with joy is a way to show love to the love of your life.

Telling your story to your kids or other loved ones will accomplish two things. For one, it will re-establish the history you share with your husband as well as bring back memories of your early times together. That shared history will reinforce your bond, remind you both of how far you've come, and create a sense of stability for your kids.

Second, speaking positively about your marriage and treating the day you met your husband as a good day in your life will help create a climate of gratitude not only in your own heart, but also in your home. Dr. Steven Toepfer, an assistant professor at Kent State University, conducted a study among his students to assess the effect of gratitude on a person's level of happiness. He found that as his students wrote letters of appreciation to significant people in their lives, they grew happier, more grateful, and more satisfied with their lives.

Use the story of meeting your husband as a way of reminding yourself of the blessing he is, and you just might find yourself feeling more satisfied and happy with the mate you have.

SHOW IT

Look for a window for conversation with your kids or someone close to you who hasn't already heard the story of how you and your husband met and

got together. It's even better if your husband is around and can hear what you tell other people about that time in your lives. Recount your meeting story with a smile on your face, and make sure to say nice things about your guy. You might get a few rolling of the eyes from the kiddos. But the story will ultimately leave everyone smiling.

> Love is what you've been
> through with somebody.
>
> JAMES THURBER

PASS IT ON

Pass the book on to your guy with a smile and a kiss. ♥

Go Ice Skating

*You have put gladness in my heart,
more than in the season that their grain
and wine increased.*

PSALM 4:7

KNOW IT

Researchers at DePauw University conducted an unusual study. They studied college yearbook photos and rated each person's smile on an intensity scale of one to ten. They found that the people with the most intense smiles were still married years later; those with weaker smiles showed a higher rate of divorce. It appears that youthful happiness might be an indicator of later marital happiness.

In any case, it doesn't take a rocket scientist to figure out that happy marriages are . . . well . . . happy marriages. Cultivating a sense of fun and levity is bound to make your marriage feel less like work and more like the joyful intimacy you so deeply want. Plus, a focus on fun is bound to keep up the feeling of happiness and anticipation you felt when you were dating. And that surely never hurt a marriage.

So maybe a youthful activity is in order. Doing something you did as kids will drain all the seriousness—and maybe even some of the stress—out of your week. And it just might strike a spark of high-school romance between you and your guy.

SHOW IT

Find an ice-skating or roller-skating rink in your city and take your hubby out for a Saturday afternoon of skating fun. The indignity of falling down will melt your grown-up composure—and give you lots of opportunities to hold hands.

> To get the full value of joy you must have someone to divide it with.
>
> MARK TWAIN

PASS IT ON

Put the book alongside your husband's favorite beverage on a coffee or end table as he's watching TV. ❤

Solicit His Opinion

Let each of you look out not only for his own interests, but also for the interests of others.

PHILIPPIANS 2:4

KNOW IT

No-Brainer Marriage Principle #208: You will not always agree. It's how you handle your disagreements that makes your marriage successful or unsuccessful.

Marriage researcher Dr. John Gottman has found that the predictors of divorce or marriage success might not be what everyone expected. Anger, for example, is not an evil in and of itself; only when it's mishandled or expressed with contempt does it become toxic to a marriage. And what does seem to indicate stability in a marriage is a partnership mentality and a willingness to accept each other's suggestions.

Of course, in order to accept each other's suggestions and opinions, you have to know what they are. As tempting as it may be to take a "me first" approach here and make sure your husband knows—and takes seriously—your opinion on every item that affects you as a couple, press the pause button on that impulse. Remember that this principle is about reciprocity and mutuality. You want your ideas heard, but you need to be willing to hear your husband's too. Besides, when you take the initiative to listen respectfully to your partner's ideas, you'll make it easier for him to do the same for you.

So make the first move by soliciting and listening to your husband's opinion on something that matters to both of you.

SHOW IT

Is there a pressing issue in your family's life right now? Maybe it's a school decision for the kids, a potential career change for you or your husband, or a major money matter. When the two of you have some free time to talk,

ask him what he thinks about that burning issue. Even if you disagree, take the time to listen and ask him why he thinks what he does. It's not against the rules to share your own thoughts, and you probably won't decide anything tonight. But the importance of this exercise is to show respect and consideration for your husband's opinion.

A man is already halfway in love with
any woman who listens to him.

BRENDAN FRANCIS

PASS IT ON

Place the book on the desk or workspace where you keep your family's important papers, in a spot where your husband will see it and know it's his turn. Include a note that says, "We're in this together—and I couldn't be happier."

Your Turn

Love never fails.

1 CORINTHIANS 13:8

On the other side of this page is one final activity, one you'll share with your husband. But before you turn the page, pause for a minute. Think back on the previous weeks or months and the activities you've completed. And ask yourself a few questions:

- Which activity in this book received the most enthusiastic response from your husband?
- Which one did you enjoy most as the giver, and which as the receiver?
- In what ways do you think your efforts to practice loving your husband have paid off in your marriage?

Now it's your turn. With the answers to the above questions in mind, think up one last activity, one more way of showing love to your spouse. Make it something specific to him, his desires and soft spots, his tastes, and something meaningful to you as well.

If you've learned anything through the course of this book, we hope it's that love put into words and actions can grow stronger each day. Sometimes our efforts might be and feel awkward; and sometimes we miss the mark a little. But when we make loving our spouse a priority, our efforts pay off.

he Middle

For this activity, the two of you will work together. Block off a little time and find a comfortable spot to talk. Take turns asking and answering the questions around the game board—and really listen to each other's answers. Share you.

Start Here

Something y have done for recently that rea showed me how mu you love me is

What do I do that makes you feel loved? Is there anything I do that makes you feel unloved?

Something I really like to do to show you how much I love you is . . .

Something I learned from working through this book with you is . . .

ink one area ur relationship t needs some rk is . . .

What do we do together that you most enjoy?